Bear

At the breathless Pole
A bear is turning round
A ball whiter
Than snow and himself.
How can you make him understand
From the depths of this Paris
That this is an old globe,
Ever more and more reduced,
Of a midnight sun.
The bear is so far away
From this closed room.
He is so different
From the familiar beasts
Who pass my door.
The bear uncomprehending, bends over
His little sun
And tries, bit by bit,
To warm it with his breath
And his dark tongue.

As if he took it
For a chilly little bear
Curled up and motionless
With tight closed eyes.

JULES SUPERVIELLE (1884–1960)
Translated from the French by Kenneth Rexroth

Lost, Stolen, Strayed

The gone dog leaves a ghost.
His bark comes to the door.
Running against our knowing
we whistle to a wish

We hear his shaking ears
and see the birch at the window
shiver. It was a bird
that fluttered sudden wings

Returning home, we see
solid delusive air
wagging a welcome dance
baring teeth in a smile

He was so very here.
Now through the hills of where
he runs—and wounds our waiting
with shams of his return

DILYS LAING (1906–1960)

Watering the Garden

When I drag the hose
toward the zucchini,
a brown striped snake uncoils
from underneath the eggplant,
gliding through the dust,
his red tongue
hotter than the sun.

I know he'll eat
the toad who lives
among the squash leaves.
I chase him through
the wire fence with water;
he comes back on drier
ground, serene as death.

How can I reach deep
in the green beans
when he might be there,
just there
where my fingers touch.
At night he slithers
through my dreams
in search of warmth.

LUCILE BLANCHARD (20th century)

The Poet Stumbles Upon the Astronomer's Orchards

Once a scholar showed me the sky.
He held up a grapefruit:
here is the sun.
He held up an orange:
this is the harvest moon.
If you watch my hands, you will see
how the sun stays in its socket,
how the earth turns, how the moon
ripens and falls and swells again.

Under an axle tree, I took my seat.
The leaves were stars,
      juggling pineapples and pears.
        What a show!
A thousand lemons are rolling through space,
avocados nudge down the rings of Jupiter
and coconuts shake the galaxy to its teeth
till the tree loses its leaves.

But there is a star in my apple when I cut it
and some hungry traveler is paring the moon away.

NANCY WILLARD (b. 1936)

Spring

I sit under the old oak,
And gaze at the white orchard,
In bloom under the full moon.
The oak purrs like a lion,
And seems to quiver and breathe.
I am startled until I
Realize that the beehive
In the hollow trunk will be
Busy all night long tonight.

KENNETH REXROTH (1905–1982)

Exclamation

Stillness
          not on the branch
in the air
          Not in the air
in the moment
          hummingbird

OCTAVIO PAZ (b. 1914)
Translated from the Spanish by Eliot Weinberger

Water Night

Night with the eyes of a horse that trembles in the
    night,
night with eyes of water in the field asleep
is in your eyes, a horse that trembles,
is in your eyes of secret water.

Eyes of shadow-water,
eyes of well-water,
eyes of dream-water.

Silence and solitude,
two little animals moon-led,
drink in your eyes,
drink in those waters.

If you open your eyes,
night opens, doors of musk,
the secret kingdom of the water opens
flowing from the center of the night.

And if you close your eyes,
a river fills you from within,
flows forward, darkens you:
night brings its wetness to beaches in your soul.

OCTAVIO PAZ (b. 1914)
Translated from the Spanish

The Premonition

Walking this field I remember
Days of another summer.
Oh that was long ago! I kept
Close to the heels of my father,
Matching his stride with half-steps
Until we came to a river.
He dipped his hand in the shallow:
Water ran over and under
Hair on a narrow wrist bone;
His image kept following after,—
Flashed with the sun in the ripple.
But when he stood up, that face
Was lost in a maze of water.

THEODORE ROETHKE (1908–1963)

Leaves

Peace to these little broken leaves,
   That strew our common ground;
That chase their tails, like silly dogs,
   As they go round and round.

For though in winter boughs are bare,
   Let us not once forget
Their summer glory, when these leaves
   Caught the great Sun in their stronger net;
And made him, in the lower air,
Tremble—no bigger than a star!

W. H. DAVIES (1870–1940)

After Akiko—"Yoru no cho ni"

for Yasuyo

In your frost white kimono
Embroidered with bare branches
I walk you home New Year's Eve.
As we pass a street lamp
A few tiny bright feathers
Float in the air. Stars form on
Your wind blown hair and you cry,
"The first snow!"

KENNETH REXROTH (1905–1982)

Snow Is Falling

Snow is falling, snow is falling.
Reaching for the storm's white stars,
Petals of geraniums stretch
Beyond the window bars.

Snow is falling, all is chaos,
Everything is in the air,
The angle of the crossroads,
The steps of the back stair.

Snow is falling, not like flakes
But as if the firmament
In a coat with many patches
Were making its descent.

As if, from the upper landing,
Looking like a lunatic,
Creeping, playing hide-and-seek,
The sky stole from the attic.

Because life does not wait,
Turn, and you find Christmas here.
And a moment after that
It's suddenly New Year.

Snow is falling, thickly, thickly.
Keeping step, stride for stride,
No less quickly, nonchalantly,
Is that time, perhaps,
Passing in the street outside?

And perhaps year follows year
Like the snowflakes falling
Or the words that follow here?

Snow is falling, snow is falling,
Snow is falling, all is chaos:
The whitened ones who pass,
The angle of the crossroads,
The dazed plants by the glass.

BORIS PASTERNAK (1890–1960)
Translated from the Russian by Jon Stallworthy and Peter France

It Has All Been Fulfilled

The roads have turned to porridge.
Across the fields I trudge.
I mash up icy mud to dough,
I plod through fudgelike sludge.

A blue-jay flies between
The wood's bare birches, scolding.
The wood, like an unfinished house,
Holds up its scaffolding.

I see between its arches
My future life revealed.
It all, to the last particle,
Has been accomplished and fulfilled.

I take my time in the wood.
Snow layers lie heavily.
The blue-jay's echo will answer me,
The world make way for me.

Where snow has thawed and earth
And sodden loam show through,
A bird is chirping mutedly
Every second or two.

The wood gives ear, as if
A musical box were played;
Repeats the bird's chirp hollowly
And waits for it to fade.

I hear, then, from the boundary fence,
Three miles off, crunching hooves
And footsteps, drips falling from trees,
And snow flopping off roofs.

BORIS PASTERNAK (1890–1960)
*Translated from the Russian by Jon Stallworthy
and Peter France*

Migrants

Birds whose punctual airways
are stairways north and south
expand their small strong lungs
to climb those annual rungs.

Before the northern growth
is green within the eye
those treaders of the sky
have wheeled to wintry earth.

They crack the brown seed-cases
of grasses, goldenrod,
last season's black-eyed Susans.

In dozens and in hundreds
with single kindred motion,
angled in intuition,
they swoop to snatch their ration
upon their northward path.

I did not know the meadow
all widowed of its green
had quite so full a pantry
for quite so many lean
invaders of my country.

DILYS LAING (1906–1960)

Waders and Swimmers

The first morning it flew out of the fog
I thought it lived there.
It floated into shore all shoulders,
all water and air. It was cold that summer.
In the white dark the sun coming up was the moon.
And then this beautiful bird,
its wings as large as a man, drawing the line
of itself out of the light behind it.
A month or more it flew out of the fog,
fished, fed, gone in a moment.

There are no blue herons in Ohio.
But one October in a park I saw a swan
lift itself from the water in singular, vertical strokes.
It got high enough to come back down wild.
It ate bread from the hand
and swallowed in long, irregular gestures.
It seemed, to a child, almost angry.
I remember what I hated
when someone tied it wing-wide to a tree.
The note nailed to its neck said this is nothing.

The air is nothing, though it rise
and fall. Another year
a bird the size of a whooping crane
flew up the Hocking—
people had never seen a bird that close
so large and white at once.
They called it their ghost and went back to their Bibles.
It stood on houses for days, lost,
smoke from the river.
In the wing-light of the dawn it must have passed

its shadow coming and going. I wish I knew.
I still worry a swan alive
through an early Ohio winter, still worry
its stuttering, clipped wings.
It rises in snow, white on white, the way
in memory one thing is confused with another.
From here to a bird that flies
with its neck folded back to its shoulders
is nothing but air, nothing but first light and summer
and water rising in a smoke of waters.

STANLEY PLUMLY (b. 1939)

Here

My footsteps in this street
Re-echo
       In another street
Where
       I hear my footsteps
Passing in this street
Where

Nothing is real but the fog

OCTAVIO PAZ (b. 1914)
Translated from the Spanish by John Frederick Nims

Dog-Walk

Over the years, my dog has worn a path
edging a vacant field.
Experience has taught her to avoid thistles and stinging
    nettle.
From thousands of walks, she's learned where plantain
    are soft—
to expect from pokeweed and piled stones,
from certain crevices,
exhilarating scents.

Leaving the house, she pulls hard on her leash—
her head into the wind, her nose and ears working.
At the pasture's high fence
she thrusts head and neck past chains
linking the paired gates,
wedging her wide shoulders farther,
farther toward the pasture's air—

until hinges, closed locks, stop her, still straining,

here, in this narrow place,
her front quarters extending as far as they can go
toward those regions she yearns for:
fenceless acreage, the lots of desire
she is denied.

She trudges slowly returning home,
her walk shambling,
her leash slack.

MARY BALAZS (b. 1939)

Dorset

The horses are taking their time under the oaks.
They shake and raise their heads
as if answering a scent
deep shade delivers to them,
then out of the shadows through thick yellow weeds
slowly washing the air of flies
with their heavy tails, they come.

They know me but keep me waiting.
There in the weeds moving like a yellow sea
under them, they stand. Yes, yes, I want to call out,
of course it's me, wade closer.
With a slight lift, first one then another
turns a disdainful head, and as if pulling
something heavy behind, drifts off
into the shade under the oaks.

DONA LUONGO STEIN (b. 1935)

Horses

Eighteen years
of hauling heavy loads,
two forgotten horses
on the lonely roads.

Eighteen years
of standing on the hard stable floor;
the horse-stall dust dimmed the sheen
their skin had all those years before.

Cringing under the whip
that stung and burned;
the straw they ate two times a day
they dearly earned.

Lashed by cold and rain one night,
the elder pressed his heavy head
against the other,
coughing as he said:

"I'm tired, brother. Eighteen years
by your side without protesting.
I'm shaking, sick, and blind,
and I need rest."

Two horses alone that night
without a future;
sold in a tavern
to a horse butcher.

Their master gave his hand
and toted up the worth
of two unhappy horses
in this wide earth.

Bargaining for one more trip
with them to haul
a last wagonload of wood,
and a cold farewell.

As it had for eighteen years
the whip cracked, and they trod
the forest path hauling wood
for the winter days ahead.

And when they came from the forest,
no need for them to eat;
they took their own flesh to the slaughter
on their own weary feet.

Two brother horses trembled
when they saw where they stood,
two long heads pressed together,
attentive to the blood.

Plain to see when the yoke was lifted
off their necks that day,
the black skin
where their manes were worn away.

Plain to hear the sound of fear
when they lay in their blood on the floor,
the wild sound of iron hooves
pounding the stony floor

like the sound of their feet on the stony street
for eighteen years,
and their heavy breath as they went—
two horses
on this lonely earth.
And now their lives are spent.

MELECH RAVITCH (1893–1976)
Translated from the Yiddish by Seymour Levitan

When I Heard the Learn'd Astronomer

When I heard the learn'd astronomer,
When the proofs, the figures, were ranged in columns
  before me,
When I was shown the charts and diagrams, to add,
  divide, and measure them,
When I sitting heard the astronomer where he lectured
  with much applause in the lecture-room,
How soon unaccountable I became tired and sick,
Till rising and gliding out I wander'd off by myself,
In the mystical moist night-air, and from time to time,
Look'd up in perfect silence at the stars.

WALT WHITMAN (1819–1892)

On the Other Side of the Poem

On the other side of the poem there is an orchard,
and in the orchard, a house with a roof of straw,
and three pine trees,
three watchmen who never speak, standing guard.

On the other side of the poem there is a bird,
yellow brown with a red breast,
and every winter he returns
and hangs like a bud in the naked bush.

On the other side of the poem there is a path
as thin as a hairline cut,
and someone lost in time
is treading the path barefoot, without a sound.

On the other side of the poem amazing things may
    happen,
even on this overcast day,
this wounded hour
that breathes its fevered longing in the windowpane.

On the other side of the poem my mother may appear
and stand in the doorway for a while lost in thought
and then call me home as she used to call me home
    long ago:
Enough play, Rokhl. Don't you see it's night?

ROKHL KORN (1898–1982)
Translated from the Yiddish by Seymour Levitan

Boy and Top

Each time he spins it,
it lands, precisely,
at the center of the world.

OCTAVIO PAZ (b. 1914)
Translated from the Spanish

Song for a Young Girl's Puberty Ceremony

I am on my way running,
I am on my way running,
Looking toward me is the edge of the world,
I am trying to reach it,
The edge of the world does not look far away,
To that I am on my way running.

ANONYMOUS
Translated from the Papago by Frances Densmore

Braiding My Sister's Hair

One strand loose, I go back, pick it up
wind it over my finger and bind it in.
Not just love keeps me at this,
to have you still, tranced beneath my hands
as if obedient to my will—we must have been
    enchanted,
you by trust, me by duty, as my hands
wound measured widths in a fall of hair
so black its thick-waved lengths shined back blue.

One braid hung behind each ear; down the back
of your scalp a white path parted hair
with a few short hairs curled where the brown skin
of your neck began. We were both children,
you three, me twelve, and it was merely my task
with your hair to help mother so you could be
outside at play. Us sisters and brothers

thought you the favored child, so agreeable
we could not be mean, yet so beloved
we could not show our love, too. Your quietude
with my care let me learn what it is to love,
how anguish in tenderness gets caught,
trained, bound as in highlights
of hair so black it shines back blue.

DONA LUONGO STEIN (b. 1935)

Learning to Swim

That summer in Tunkhannuk the cold stream
barked, dogs herding over stones. Behind me,
wading with a switch of willow in your hand,
you drove me out: large father
with your balding, sun-ripe head, quicksilver

smiles. I wavered over pebbles,
small, white curds, and listened into fear:
the falls that sheared the stream close by,
the gargle and basalt boom.
"It's safe," you said. "Now go ahead and swim."

I let it go, dry-throated, lunging.
Currents swaddled me from every side,
my vision reeling through the upturned sky.
Half dazed and flailing in a whelm of cries,
I felt your big hand father me ashore.

JAY PARINI (b. 1948)

Grandfather Talk

Are our grandfathers
ever so wise and majestic
as mahogany clocks

That stand tall,
tocking away in all
the living rooms
of dying time?

Mine was old and bent
who shuffled with pain
into his final days.

A gentle man
whose hands (like my father's)
were strong and flour-caked,

Who looked at me
with great sad eyes
as he, a baker man, handed me
a white-dusted nickel
for the week.

"Some day, Billy, someday
you will understand"
were the only words
he ever spoke or those
I can recall

Words that taunt
me even now
as a grandfather clock
swings its tongue
in syncopated talk

And I keep waiting
for the meaning.

WILLIAM S. COHEN (b. 1940)

Untitled

Do not grieve, little birds,
Over the falling blossoms:
They're not to blame, it's the wind
Who loosens and scatters the petals.
Spring is leaving us.
Don't hold it against her.

SONG SUN (1493–1582)
Translated from the Korean by Peter H. Lee

Untitled

Were you to ask me what I'd wish to be
In the world beyond this world,
I would answer, a pine tree, tall and hardy
On the highest peak of Mt. Pongnae,
And to be green, alone, green,
When snow fills heaven and earth.

SŎNG SAM-MUN (1418–1456)
Translated from the Korean by Peter H. Lee

Number 5—December

Nobody knows me
when I go round
late at night
scratching on windows
& whispering in hallways
looking for someone
who loves me in the daytime
to take me in
at night

DAVID HENDERSON (b. 1942)

Ghost Crab

Side stepping great issues, she minces
no words. She knows what's good
for her and stays hidden until
the temperature of the dune goes
down. More legs are better than two

and being above sand
on hinged knees is best. Among beach peas
and poverty grass, her delicate shades blend.
She disappears except for shy eyes

out there on stalks swiveling
after you. Imagine yourself
so constructed: your whole skeleton
a shell to protect your heart
when you were young
with nobody to love
the only sign, a crabbed trail
crossing itself the next morning.

DONA LUONGO STEIN (b. 1935)

Lonesome Boy Blues

Oh nobody's a long time
Nowhere's a big pocket
To put little
Pieces of nice things that
Have never really happened
To anyone except
Those people who were lucky enough
Not to get born

Oh lonesome's a bad place
To get crowded into
With only
Yourself riding back and forth
On
A blind white horse
Along an empty road meeting
All your
Pals face to face

Oh nobody's a long long time

KENNETH PATCHEN (1911–1972)

Recess

from REALMS OF GOLD

I used to think
the cover of a book
was a door I could pull shut
after me,
that I was as safe
between pages
as between the clean sheets
of my bed at home.
The children in those books
were not like me.
They had the shine
of bravery or luck,
and their stories had endings.
But when Miss Colton called
"Yoo Hoo, Third Grade,"
and I had to come running,
the book suddenly
slippery under my arm, sometimes
those children ran with me.

LINDA PASTAN (b. 1932)

I

I want to play
boys and girls
I want to play
come here
we're going to jump
run and climb
over walls
and sing
do a lot of
things
make a lot of
noise

Start the rocks
flying
hear them bounce
kick
hard
on the sidewalks

Destroy
all the flowers
break the pots
Frighten the
hens
so that they will sing
with us

Let the dogs
howl
let them bark
let the birds
sing
let the cats
jump
and let them all
laugh at us

Let's play
boys and girls until
our hot souls
are tired
and when we

can't lift
our arms any longer
and our legs
are worn out
we'll yell
at the moon:
        Look moon
this is playing!

FRANCISCA
(NELLIE CAMPOBELLO, b. 1909?)
Translated from the Spanish by Langston Hughes

Walking the Trestle

They are all behind you, grinning,
with their eyes like dollars, their shouts
of *dare you, dare you, dare you*
broken by the wind. You squint ahead
where the rusty trestle wavers into sky
like a pirate's plank. And sun shines
darkly on the Susquehanna, forty feet
below. You stretch your arms
to the sides of space and walk
like a groom down that bare aisle.
Out in the middle, you turn to wave
and see their faces breaking like bubbles,
the waves beneath you flashing coins,
and all around you, chittering cables,
birds, and the bright air clapping.

JAY PARINI (b. 1948)

Watching on the Railroad

When the water pipe below the farm
Was still intact, routing a bluff-side spring
Onto the riprap of the C & O,
I never dared jump on the long black trains
Heaped with coal,
Despite their pausing for the signal at Holcomb Rock.
The long hard run of track pointing in each direction
Away from home: Ohio to the west
And Chesapeake to the east, faded
To vanishing point.
Men walked the tracks then,
Mostly blacks from Coleman Falls;
Now gardeners in town
With golden Hamilton watches
And Buddha-like faces at the bus stops.

Their shirtless backs shone in the sun
As they put down their picks
And rinsed the dull tin cup
Three or four times before drinking.

I hid behind the elephant-skinned beech
Twenty paces down and listened to them rail
About the heat, and their work, and the ache
In their backs;
And then when they had finished,
I watched them walk away on the sleepers
Until they sank back down
Through the eye of the tracks'
Distant steel.

CHARD DeNIORD (b. 1952)

Monkey

from A BESTIARY

Monkeys are our relatives.
On observing their habits
Some are ashamed of monkeys,
Some deny the relation,
Some are ashamed of themselves.
They throw coconuts at us.

KENNETH REXROTH (1905–1982)

Steelhead

The day I landed my first steelhead
from the Chehalis,
I saw a crow
zigzagging across Damitio's field
like no other crow has done before.

ROBERT SUND (b. 1926)

The Family Car

When I was a kid we always had big cars:
Pontiacs, Buicks, an Oldsmobile Rocket.
Each year the bodies looked the same
but the grills got chromier and meaner looking.
With Father behind the wheel, Mother watching
    the road,
my brother and I assigned to our life-time seats in back,
our faces were painted on the toy windows.
In the hot Texas summers people walking in the
    filmy heat
seemed to float above the melting asphalt
while we cruised in air conditioning behind tinted glass.
It was quiet in there with the doors locked,
the windows sealed. From my seat in the right rear
I watched the world fan by.
This was life. This was certainty. This was big car
    roominess.

TOM ABSHER (b. 1938)

At Our House

—to Meg

Because everything
we did on paper
got crumpled up
and thrown away

or,
if it was a secret,
read,

we stopped trusting paper.

You drew your skinny angels
on the rough, dark boards
of the garage

and I wrote,
as far back on the furnace pipe
as I could reach

March 10, 1948. Grandpa is dead.

JUDITH HEMSCHEMEYER (b. 1935)

The Horseman

My grandfather owned
The last livery stable
In Long Prairie, Minnesota.
He kept the workhorses,
The Shires and Clydesdales
That they used to use
For logging, until the last
Farmer got a Ford truck
And waved at my grandfather
As he stood by his stable.
He sold the horses; the
Barn went for lumber.
And the old man went
Home from the livery stable
For the last time. He bought
A Ford and learned to drive it.
But he would never start it
Without flicking invisible reins,
And when he braked, he always
Closed his eyes and whispered, "Whoa."

GRETCHEN SCHOL (b. 1963)

Plea

To my friend
who can no longer see
animals in the clouds

and takes it
as a sign of madness:

Hang on. Keep watch.

They must be gathering now
over the Pacific,

great, soft herds of elephants,
cirrous alligators
and horses being pulled apart

with no pain.

JUDITH HEMSCHEMEYER (b. 1935)

Body Surfing

It's my father who takes me in over my head.
For once I let him hold me to his soft white belly and
    hairy chest
leaving my mother on shore.
I'm high in his arms
but the waves are higher.
An explosion above.
A pull.
Then we both go under.
He won't let go.

This is where I learned to love deep water,
to flirt with the undertow, seek out the breakers
that ripped off my bathing cap,
scraped me on sand,
sent me slamming into the knees to strangers.

KATHLEEN AGUERO (b. 1949)

Empty Head

An idea came
Into my head
So slender
So slight
An idea came
Fleetingly
Fearfully
Came to alight
It wheeled about
Stretched itself out
An idea came
That I wanted to stay
But it brushed my hand
And taking its flight
Through my fingers
Slipped away.

MALICK FALL (b. 1920)
Translated from the French by John Reed and Clive Wake

The Dirty-Billed Freeze Footy

Remember that Saturday morning
Mother forgot the word gull?

We were all awake but still in bed
and she called out, "Hey kids!

What's the name of that bird that eats garbage
and stands around in cold water on the beach?"

And you, the quick one, the youngest daughter
piped right back: "A dirty-billed freeze footy!"

And she laughed till she was weak,
until it hurt her. And you had done it:

reduced our queen to warm and helpless rubble.

And the rest of the day, baking or cleaning
or washing our hair until it squeaked,

whenever she caught sight of you
it would start all over again.

JUDITH HEMSCHEMEYER (b. 1935)

The Spider

I'm told that the spider
Has coiled up inside her
Enough silky material
To spin an aerial
One-way track
to the moon and back;
Whilst I
Cannot even catch a fly.

FRANK COLLYMORE (1893–1980)

There Is a Tree That Stands

There is a tree that stands
And bows beside the road.
All its birds have fled away,
Leaving not a bird.

The tree, abandoned to the storm,
Stands there all alone:
Three birds east, and three birds west—
The others south have flown.

To my mother then, I say,
"If you won't meddle, please,
I'll turn myself into a bird
Right before your eyes.

"All winter, I'll sit on the tree
And sing him lullabies,
I'll rock him and console him
With lovely melodies."

Tearfully, my mother says,
"Don't take any chances.
God forbid, up in the tree
You'll freeze among the branches."

"Mother, what a shame to spoil
Your eyes with tears," I said,
Then, on the instant, I transformed
Myself into a bird.

My mother cried, "Oh, Itsik, love . . .
In the name of God,
Take a little scarf with you
To keep from catching cold.

"And dear, put your galoshes on,
The winter's cold and aching.
Be sure to wear your fleece-lined cap;
Woe's me, my heart is breaking.

"And, pretty fool, be sure to take
Your woolen underwear
And put it on, unless you mean
To lie a corpse somewhere."

I try to fly, but I can't move . . .
Too many, many things
My mother's piled on her weak bird
And loaded down my wings.

I look into my mother's eyes
And, sadly, there I see
The love that won't let me become
The bird I want to be.

ITSIK MANGER (1901–1969)
Translated from the Yiddish by Leonard Wolf

Vision

I saw myself when I shut my eyes:
space, space
where I am and am not.

OCTAVIO PAZ (b. 1914)
Translated from the Spanish

Runner

I am running so slowly
I have forgotten the rules
of this life. A lily
spreads itself open
above its pad in the river.
Brown lines move toward
the eye of a duck
sucking at water. Rocks
turn slowly into
their own beds of sand.

I have been running so long
I have forgotten the season.
Birch, alder, shed and die
then sprout and bloom again.
In gasped breathing
at the edge of exhaustion,
my feet do not touch sand,
they sink
steadily deeper
into the next century.

DONA LUONGO STEIN (b. 1935)

Untitled

pro basketball players
live in bat caves
upside down
hotel rooms
minds pointing
to darkness . . .

TOM MESCHERY (b. 1938)

As It Should Be

A black hand supports
the white body of a fallen teammate.

The ball that scored the winning goal
was placed in motion by a gray hand.

The sweat pouring from our bodies
is neither black nor white.

TOM MESCHERY (b. 1938)

The Last Poem

When
      the game has ended
      and the roar of the crowd
      has faded into the past
      and only the cleaning brooms
      click-clack echoes
      on the empty rows of seats
      drumming through
      the dim-lit concrete corridors
      of the stadium what
then?

TOM MESCHERY (b. 1938)

A Man

While fighting for his country, he lost an arm
and was suddenly afraid:
"From now on, I shall only be able to do things by
    halves.
I shall reap half a harvest.
I shall be able to play either the tune
or the accompaniment on the piano,
but never both parts together.
I shall be able to bang with only one fist
on doors, and worst of all
I shall only be able to half hold
my love close to me.
There will be things I cannot do at all,
applaud for example,
at shows where everyone applauds."

From that moment on, he set himself to do everything
    with twice as much enthusiasm.
And where the arm had been torn away
a wing grew.

NINA CASSIAN (b. 1924)
Translated from the Romanian by Roy MacGregor-Hastie

Spring Poem in the Skagit Valley

The birds are going the other way now,
passing houses as they go.

And geese fly
        back
    and forth
        across the valley,
        getting ready.

The sound of geese in the distance
    is wonderful:
        in our minds
        we rise up
        and move on.

ROBERT SUND (b. 1926)

To Satch
(American Gothic)

Sometimes I feel like I will *never* stop
Just go on forever
Till one fine mornin'
I'm gonna reach up and grab me a handfulla stars
Swing out my long lean leg
And whip three hot strikes burnin' down the heavens
And look over at God and say
How about that!

SAMUEL ALLEN
(PAUL VESEY, b. 1917)

Index of Authors

Absher, Tom   67

Aguero, Kathleen   71

Allen, Samuel   85

Anonymous   47

Balazs, Mary   37

Blanchard, Lucile   18

Cassian, Nina   83

Cohen, William S.   51

Collymore, Frank   74

Davies, W. H.   26

deNiord, Chard   63

Fall, Malick   72

Francisca   59

Hemschemeyer, Judith   68, 70, 73

Henderson, David   55

Korn, Rokhl   44

Laing, Dilys   17, 32

Manger, Itsik   75

Meschery, Tom   80, 81, 82

Mistral, Gabriela   12

Olivares Figueroa, R.   1

Parini, Jay   50, 62

Pastan, Linda   58

Pasternak, Boris   28, 30

Patchen, Kenneth   9, 57

Paz, Octavio   4, 8, 22, 23, 36, 46, 78

Plumly, Stanley   34

Ravitch, Melech   40

Reisen, Abraham   3

Rexroth, Kenneth   6, 21, 27, 65

Rich, Adrienne   11

Roethke, Theodore   10, 25

Schol, Gretchen   69

Simpson, Louis   2

Sŏng Sam-mun   54

Song Sun   53

Stein, Dona Luongo   39, 48, 56, 79

Sund, Robert   66, 84

Supervielle, Jules   15

Turner, W. J.   5

Wasiczko, Donna   7

Whitman, Walt   43

Willard, Nancy   20

Yungch'ŏn, Master   14

Index of Titles

After Akiko—"Yoru no cho ni"	27
As It Should Be	81
At Our House	68
Aunt Jennifer's Tigers	11
Bananas	7
Bat, The	10
Bear	15
Body Surfing	71
Boy and Top	46
Braiding My Sister's Hair	48
Deer, from A Bestiary	6
Dirty-Billed Freeze Footy, The	73
Dog-Walk	37
Dorset	39
Empty Head	72
Exclamation	22
Family Car, The	67
Frogs	2
Ghost Crab	56
Grandfather Talk	51
Here	36
Horseman, The	69

Horses	40
I	59
India	5
It Has All Been Fulfilled	30
Last Poem, The	82
Last Street, The	3
Learning to Swim	50
Leaves	26
Little Girl That Lost a Finger, The	12
Lonesome Boy Blues	57
Lost, Stolen, Strayed	17
Magical Mouse, The	9
Man, A	83
Migrants	32
Monkey, from A Bestiary	65
Number 5—December	55
On the Other Side of the Poem	44
Plea	70
Poet Stumbles Upon the Astronomer's Orchards, The	20
Premonition, The	25
Proverb	4
Recess, from Realms of Gold	58
Reversible	8
Runner	79
Snow Is Falling	28
Song for a Young Girl's Puberty Ceremony	47

Song of the Comet   14
Sower, The   1
Spider, The   74
Spring   21
Spring Poem in the Skagit Valley   84
Steelhead   66
There Is a Tree That Stands   75
To Satch (American Gothic)   85
Untitled (Sŏng Sam-mun)   54
Untitled (Song Sun)   53
Untitled (Tom Meschery)   80
Vision   78
Waders and Swimmers   34
Walking the Trestle   62
Watching on the Railroad   63
Water Night   23
Watering the Garden   18
When I Heard the Learn'd Astronomer   43

Index of First Lines

A black hand supports   81
An idea came   72
And a clam caught my little finger,   12
Are our grandfathers   51
At the breathless Pole   15
Aunt Jennifer's tigers prance across a screen,   11
Because everything   68
Birds whose punctual airways   32
By day the bat is cousin to the mouse.   10
Deer are gentle and graceful   6
Do not grieve, little birds,   53
Each time he spins it,   46
Eighteen years   40
I am on my way running,   47
I am running so slowly   79
I am the magical mouse   9
I saw myself when I shut my eyes: 78
I sit under the old oak,   21
I used to think   58
I want to play   59
I'm told that the spider   74
In space   8

In your frost white kimono   27

It may be   7

It's my father who takes me in over my head.   71

Monkeys are our relatives.   65

Mud in a still puddle: 4

My footsteps in this street   36

My grandfather owned   69

Night with the eyes of a horse that trembles in the night,   23

Nobody knows me   55

Oh nobody's a long time   57

On a white field,   1

On the other side of the poem there is an orchard,   44

Once a scholar showed me the sky.   20

One strand loose, I go back, pick it up   48

Over the years, my dog has worn a path   37

Peace to these little broken leaves,   26

pro basketball players   80

Remember that Saturday morning   73

Side stepping great issues, she minces   56

Snow is falling, snow is falling.   28

Sometimes I feel like I will never stop   85

Stillness   22

That summer in Tunkhannuk the cold stream   50

The birds are going the other way now,   84

The day I landed my first steelhead   66

The first morning it flew out of the fog   34

The gone dog leaves a ghost.   17

The horses are taking their time under the oaks.   39

The last street of the town;   3

The roads have turned to porridge.   30

The storm broke, and it rained,   2

There is a castle by the Eastern Sea,   14

There is a tree that stands   75

They are all behind you, grinning,   62

They hunt, the velvet tigers in the jungle,   5

To my friend   70

Walking this field I remember   25

Were you to ask me what I'd wish to be   54

When   82

When I drag the hose   18

When I heard the learn'd astronomer,   43

When I was a kid we always had big cars: 67

When the water pipe below the farm   63

While fighting for his country, he lost an arm   83